FINCHES AS A NEW PET

MORGAN KELVEY

CONTENTS

W9-AWO-045

Photos by: Dr. Herbert R. Axelrod, Cliff Bickford, Michael DeFreitas, Michael Gilroy, Eric Ilasenko, Kruger National Park, Harry Lacey, Horst Mayer, R. & V. Moat, Irene & Michael Morocombe, Robert Pearcy, T. Tilford, John Tyson, Vogelpark Walsrode.

T.F.H. Publications, Inc.
One TFH Plaza
Third and Union Avenues
Neptune City, NJ 07753

ISBN 0-86622-620-6

www.tfh.com

Introducing Finches

As a broad group, finches and finch-like birds are kept in greater numbers than any other birds. This is because they are small, quiet, often colorful, and they are not destructive to their accommodation. Many are inexpensive birds available to birdkeepers, and a number may live to reach the ripe old age of twenty years under favorable conditions, though ten is perhaps a more realistic average. A few species are extremely well established in captivity - so much so that they are regarded as being domesticated (the canary varieties and the Zebra Finch for example). Finally, most have a pleasant song, with some ranking among the most melodious of any bird species.

WHAT IS A FINCH?

In ornithology the term "finch" refers to any member of the family Fringillidae - the sparrows and their like. However, in aviculture (birdkeeping), the word is used in a much looser sense. It embraces a whole multitude of species that are small perching songbirds which eat seed. Such birds are often called hardbills which distinguishes them from the so-called softbills - those birds whose diet is essentially of insects and fruits.

The terms hardbill and softbill should not be adheared to literally. Nearly all

A characteristic feature of the Common Waxbill, *Estrilda astrild*, is the crimson eye streak which starts from the base of the beak and runs over and also below the eye to the ear.

"finches" require green- and softfoods as part of their diet, as well as seeds. Some will also require insectivorous foods in addition to seeds and greenfoods at all times.

Finches and finch-like birds are found throughout the world from the frozen wastes of Siberia to the dense tropical jungles of Afro-Asia, and to the arid deserts of Australia. Some are very easy to keep, while others are very delicate and not suited to the novice birdkeeper. It is therefore essential that they are selected with consideration for many factors.

In this small book all aspects of keeping finches as pets in the home or garden are discussed. The text is of course basic, but detailed enough for you to select, accommodate, and maintain a small collection of these birds.

Lavender Waxbill, *Estrilda caerulescens*. The beautiful coloration of the Lavender Waxbill, of course, gives this bird its name.

Selecting Stock

If you have decided that you wish to keep a number of finches, but have never kept birds before, there are a number of considerations you must make before you can go about the task of acquiring stock.

CAGE OR AVIARY?

There are advantages and disadvantages of both cages and aviaries. Aviaries will of course cost considerably more to erect, space is required to locate one or more aviaries, and in areas of colder climates an indoor shelter or birdroom is also required. The time needed to maintain aviaries is greater than that needed for a number of cages. Several cages can be kept within the confines of a home where no extra light or heating costs will be incurred.

The number of species that can be bred will be significantly higher if they are accommodated in an aviary.

That this Zebra Finch, *Poephila guttata*, is a male is evident from the orange cheek patches, the striping across the throat and breast and the flanks with white spots.

Such birds will also be hardier once acclimatized to the outdoor weather. However, most of the popular species that beginners commence with are so domesticated that they will breed in cages. If only two or three birds are to be kept as house pets, a large cage will no doubt be suitable. In general, with a few exceptions, foreign finches are not ideal candidates as caged house pets. They require a larger amount of flying room than the domesticated finch. The commercial foreign finch cage is hardly a suitable home for any finch unless it is given the same sort of room freedom one would normally give to a budgerigar, or similar parrot-like species.

YOUR BIRDKEEPING OBJECTIVES

The reasons one wishes to keep finches will influence the choice of birds to begin with. In broad terms, birdkeepers can be divided into the following groups:

Society Finch, *Lonchura domestica.* **Society Finches are very eager breeders. When housed with other breeding finches, they often assist in incubating the eggs. Very often, breeders will put the eggs from very rare finches under the Society to raise as its own.**

1. Those who wish to specialize in breeding a single species, or a small number of species which are similar in geographic habitat, or visual type.

2. Those who breed primarily to produce exhibition stock. The number of species available to this group is limited to those birds which have an established record of captive breeding.

3. Those who breed for color mutations. Here the number of species is even more restricted.

4. Those who keep birds for their color and singing ability. Here the object is not primarily to breed birds, but to enjoy their beauty. The main consideration with mixed collections is that the birds are compatible.

5. Those who wish to own birds of superb singing ability. The choice of species for these people is very limited.

Although many finches have a sweet song it is the Roller canary that is the maestro of melody, along with one or two other canaries and various hybrid birds.

While many birdkeepers may have more than one objective in mind it is best if you can identify the main reason you wish to keep these birds, then commence with those best suited to this.

HARDINESS

Under this heading comes a few important aspects that are crucial to your selection process. Some species come from tropical climates and may never be suited to winter in the cold climates of England, Canada, or most American states. If they are kept in aviaries they must be provided with background heat in the winter months - not necessarily high temperatures, but sufficient to keep the air a few degrees above freezing. Just how warm will be reflected by the species and its history. The history of a bird is related to where it was from. For example, a Zebra Finch bred from generations of birds kept in outdoor aviaries will probably be far hardier than those bred from indoor caged stock. If your birds are to be kept in an aviary then try to obtain aviary bred stock. Likewise, home bred stock from a cage or aviary is better than that which has been taken from the wild. Indoor stock requires careful acclimatization before it can be maintained over a winter in an aviary, even if the species is regarded as being hardy.

Hardiness also relates to the bird's ability to accept captivity. This is more applicable to wild

The Star Finch, *Neochmia ruficauda*, is one of the best aviary birds, being inoffensive to other birds, it is very lively and will breed well in mixed company or in a colony.

7

Orange Weaver, *Euplectes orix francisciana.* Weavers are fairly aggressive birds and should not be housed with small waxbills or Australian Grassfinches. The male weaver attains his beautiful coloring during the breeding season.

caught imported stock. Some species are far more delicate than others, and can quickly die if subjected to stress, or any conditions that reduce their will to eat, or simply to survive. Delicate birds are best housed in their own quarters until they are eating well and are accustomed to the sounds of their new environment. To place freshly acquired birds into an existing mixed aviary or cage collection is very unwise. All birds should be isolated initially so they have time to build up their strength. Two or three weeks is the normal time span for basic quarantine.

WHERE TO PURCHASE FROM

The source of your first birds depends on what is desired from the birds. If they are to be kept as pets, a local pet shop will normally have a selection of popular species. Shop around. If they are to be exhibition birds, then again your pet shop will usually be the source. You may wish to purchase birds that are not well established in captivity, in this case it is best to look in the various bird magazines of your country. If you are able to collect the birds personally this is much better than purchasing through mail order because you can see what you are buying.

Another source of the lesser seen species is a large bird show. At this type of show you not only see a wide selection of birds, but they are often attended by specialist dealers and importers with stock for sale. If you plan to breed and exhibit species such as canaries,

Zebra Finches or Gouldians, such birds are best obtained from established breeders. You will need quality stock of known genotype. These birds will be more costly than pet birds, but in the long run they are the less costly option. Bird exhibitions are the best place to commence looking for breeding and show stock. At such venues all of the color mutations will be seen, and you can make contact with local breeders from your area. The various specialty and general foreign finch clubs who have booths at these shows will be able to advise you of members in your area.

If you are simply purchasing birds as pets, bear in mind that the males have a sweeter song, and in some species will be the more colorful. Overall, however, the sexes in finches and finch-like birds look much the same.

SELECTING HEALTHY BIRDS

Clearly, you should obtain healthy birds, which are not difficult to select if a common sense approach is taken. The following are pointers to choosing healthy specimens:

1. The birds should be active. When you approach their cage they will flutter about - even if they are feeling unwell. With this in mind stay a few feet away and look for any that are perched with their head tucked into its shoulders. A sick bird sits with its feathers fluffed up and perched on both legs. When the rest of the stock is active it is not a good sign to see one bird sleeping. If it is sleeping with both feet grasping the perch it is probably not feeling well (healthy birds sleep on one foot). If its head is dropped forward this is a further sign of ill health. If it is on the cage floor and huddled in a corner it may indicate ill health, or that it

Although not overly endowed with color, the Owl Finch, *Poephila bichenovii*, is a very attractive bird of distinct and sharp contrasts.

Bronze Mannikin, *Lonchura cucullata*. The Bronze Mannikin is a neat, trim, and well-groomed bird. It is a very popular aviary bird because it is unobtrusive which is not common for mannikins.

is a recent arrival in the store and is still very nervous. Pass over such birds.

2. The eyes should be round, clear, and sparkling. Any that are dull, hazy looking, or weeping, have a problem, or are recovering from one.

3. The nostrils should not be swollen or discharging any liquid.

4. The mandibles of the beak should be neatly aligned and in no way damaged, either of which would make feeding difficult.

5. The vent area should be clean and show no signs of either congealed fecal matter or staining.

6. The feathers should be neat, tight, and smart looking. The odd broken feather is not a problem - it will soon be replaced. Bald areas indicate either feather plucking or a skin parasite. Either way such birds are not for you. Young birds fresh from the nest may have been denuded of head feathers by the hen while they were in the nest. Such feathers

will regrow but even so there is no need for you to start off with such birds.

7. If you purchase very young stock try to view it eating hard seed, or have the seller assure you it is fully independent of its parents.

The foregoing are points applicable directly to the birds, but their accommodation can indicate if problems might be in a state of incubation. For example, if their cage is overstocked this is a bad sign. If the floor is full of unremoved fecal matter, and if the perches are badly stained and unduly worn, this also indicates the owner is very lax on hygiene. Such stock is at a much greater risk to illness than those maintained in well cleaned, and low stocked cages or aviaries. If you have any doubts as to the general standard of cleanliness maintained by the seller do yourself a favor and seek another supplier.

A few final points worthy of mention when thinking of purchasing finches are that you should try to select birds of similar size if they are to be housed together. If you plan to breed the birds in a mixed collection aviary, select species of differing colors and nesting habits. This will avoid unnecessary bickering during the breeding season.

Be sure that any finches that are indigenous to your country or state can be legally kept under captive conditions. Most cannot unless they carry closed metal rings showing they were bred from existing captive

Peter's Twinspot, *Hypargos niveoguttatus*. Twinspots are extremely rare in aviculture, but nearly every bird fancier who keeps rare birds should attempt to own some of them.

stocks. Some species may be illegal to keep under any circumstances - the fines for attempting to do so can be very hefty, so check this aspect with your local pet store or game department.

Accommodation

There are two potential ways in which you can house your finches: a cage or an aviary. Essentially, the difference between the two is that an aviary is an outside structure while a cage is kept indoors. Usually, an aviary is much larger than a cage, but this need not always be so. A large indoor cage could be larger than a small aviary, but it would then normally be called an indoor flight.

CAGES

There are numerous options open to you if you select a cage as a home for your finches. It should be added that as finches are usually very social birds, you are recommended to always keep two or more together so that they have the company of their own kind. A cage may be an all metal structure, one of epoxy resin coated metals, or of wood and metal. Pet shops will stock the following types:

1. The ornate metal cage sold for canaries and other small finches. These are usually only suited to keeping two birds in them. They are actually not a very good choice unless they are very large - and these tend to be expensive. The tall circular models may look good, but they are the least satisfactory for keeping any birds in. Avians prefer good length in which they can flutter from one end to the other. Fancy metal cages are usually sold on the strength of their appearance, rather than on their merits for keeping birds in.

2. Wooden stock cages. These may be in unpainted or painted wood. Stock cages are made in a variety of sizes, and most include a means to divide them into smaller units if required. This is done by inserting wooden or plastic divider panels. You can also purchase wooden stock and breeding cages in tiers.

3. Metal panels. These enable you to assemble an all metal cage of a size suited to your needs. Be sure that the panels are of narrow bar size suited to small finches.

An alternative to the ready made cage is to design and build your own, then purchase the needed finch front from your pet store, or one of the specialty companies that stock a wide range of sizes. Such companies advertise in the cage and aviary bird magazines of your country.

Unless you are going to give your birds the freedom of your living or other room, the golden rule is to provide a cage that allows them the maximum amount of flying space. This also gives you a better opportunity to furnish the cage in a natural and attractive manner. Whatever your choice, be sure the wire front is suited to finches; small finches can escape through the wider bars on standard budgerigar cages.

FLIGHT CAGES

If birds are to be housed indoors then the flight cage is easily the best way to house your pets. It need not be an ugly looking structure, and it can be tailor made to fit into a convenient alcove or space. You can now purchase such structures, but usually people design and make their own using one of the natural woods for the frame, or staining white timbers. You can purchase plastic coated weld wire mesh so the whole flight blends in nicely with your home. Such flights can have planted shrubs in them as well as natural

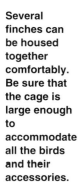

Several finches can be housed together comfortably. Be sure that the cage is large enough to accommodate all the birds and their accessories.

branches. You can keep more finches in such structures, and take pleasure in the thought that they will be much happier than in a small cage.

The back wall of such a flight could feature a mural depicting a forest or other natural scene. Be sure the floor is covered with a material that is easily wiped clean.

AVIARIES

A well designed and furnished aviary can be a beautiful addition to a garden, especially when stocked with colorful birds that may also have a nice song. You can purchase a range of standard aviaries that simply need to be assembled, or you can purchase manufacturer built ones. An alternative is to erect a flight from an unused garden shed, or an existing outbuilding not in use. Most aviculturists eventually build/have built, one or more aviaries to their own design. The important considerations are as follows:

1. The site. Ideally, the flight part of the aviary structure should gain some benefit from the early morning sunshine. It should not be located under overhanging tree branches as these pose many potential problems. Falling autumn leaves, the droppings of wild birds, the high number of insects in the summer months, and the presence of fungi, are all health hazards that are unneeded. However, a site that gains protection from winds and driving rains is very useful, so trees in the background can be beneficial. The site should be within view of your home. If it is close by, you can provide services, such

Cape Weaver, *Hyphanternis capensis*. The Cape Weaver is the most golden of the group of yellow weavers. It is altogether a very attractive bird, but is not commonly seen.

as electric, water and sewage, at a low cost.

2. The aviary floor. Bare earth is not the best choice simply because it will become saturated rather quickly with your birds' droppings (as well as those of wild birds). It is difficult to keep clean. Gravel chippings are a low cost option as they can be hosed and raked over each week. Concrete slabs are another possibility. They are easy to lay and easy to clean. A concrete floor takes longer to lay, but provides ease of cleaning and prevents burrowing animals from

gaining access to the flight. You can mix a coloring powder in with the concrete to make it more visually attractive. Do not forget to build a slight slope into the floor, away from the shelter, so rainwater easily runs away.

3. The aviary flight. This is best if of pre-made panels. These allow you to extend at a later date. The weld wire will need a small hole size of 1.25x1.25cm ($\frac{1}{2}$ x$\frac{1}{2}$in) if you wish to prevent mice from entering and very small finches from escaping. The larger size of 2.5x1.25cm (1x$\frac{1}{2}$in) is less costly but quite adequate if you do not have a rodent or snake problem in your garden.

4. A safety porch should be added to the flight so that you can enter this without risk of the birds flying past you and away.

5. The aviary panels can be mounted onto the slab or concrete floor, or onto a small wall. This looks esthetically pleasing and enables you to have good height to the flight if using 1.8m (6ft) panels. The height of the flight should

Diamond Firetail, *Emblema guttata*. The Diamond Firetail originates from Australia and is larger than most other grassfinches. When these birds are overcrowded in an aviary, they become quite aggressive.

always be in excess of 1.8m (6ft) for the best visual effect. The width and length of the flight can never be too large but 91cm (36in) would be the minimum width and 1.8 m (6ft) the minimum length in order to accommodate a few pairs of finches. A false roof panel of weld wire is useful if there are predatory birds in your area. It prevents them landing on the aviary roof and grasping any finches that might be clinging to the wire in fear. It likewise prevents cats and rodents from doing the same.

6. The Shelter or Birdroom. The main essential of this is that it be light and draftproof. The birds will enter the shelter via a pop hole that should be fitted with a landing platform. It is also useful to have a sliding door so the birds can be retained in the shelter (or

aviary) if you wish. Arrange it so you can open and close the door without the need to enter the shelter or the flight. A rod or a cable mechanism to the flight exterior will give you this facility.

In a shelter all of the internal space is in effect an indoor flight. In a birdroom the space is divided between the indoor flight and a working/storage area for yourself. The birdroom is thus the more practical

Red Headed Lady Gouldian, *Chloebia gouldiae mirabilis*. One of the most vividly colored birds of the world is the Lady Gouldian Finch. The most accurate description of the Lady Gould would be to say it includes all the better colors of the rainbow plus a few more.

option for most aviculturists. Allow yourself as much working space as possible, you will be surprised just how quickly you find yourself short of this. There are many utilities that are worth having in a birdroom and among these are lighting for working when the winter months come. Heating will also be appreciated by you as well as the birds, however, only have this to a low level otherwise the birds will become chilled when they fly into the flight. Avoid heaters that use fuels which could release toxic fumes. The heat should be controlled by a thermostat. A dimmer fitted to the lights is very useful, and a means by which the birds will not be startled by being plunged into

sudden darkness.

An ionizer is well recommended. It will remove most of the dust and airborne bacteria. It is economical to run and is stocked by most good pet shops or avicultural suppliers. Most can be plugged into any electrical socket, or even a light fitting, depending on the model size.

You are also strongly recommended to visit a number of aviary owners in your area before you erect your own aviary. You will profit from talks with these people and avoid the pitfalls they may have experienced. You will also find that where aviaries and shelters are concerned it really does pay to use the best materials.

Feeding

The basic diet of most finch and finch-like birds consists of various seeds. This is supplemented with numerous insects and softfoods - meaning fruits and berries. While some finches can get by on an almost all seed diet, this does not mean that such a regimen is good for them. There are many species that must have the varied foods mentioned in order to remain in good health. All species should have this variety when they are breeding.

Other than their basic diet, your finches will need fresh water available at all times. They may appear to drink very little of this, especially if they are partaking of fruits and greenfoods, but it must still be there for them. Another essential to birds, especially those kept in your home, is grit. Birds do not have teeth, and they crush their food in two stages. First, they dehusk the seeds with their beaks, and may crush the seed as well. It then passes into the digestive system where it mixes with minerals (grit) they have picked up from the ground. These help to grind the food into a paste-like constituency with the aid of powerful intestinal muscles.

It is important that the grit be offered in a size that the birds can swallow. Be sure to ask for finch grit in

Pied Zebra Finch, *Poephila guttata.* **All finches should have a well-balanced and varied diet. Fresh fruits and vegetables in addition to a good seed mixture will provide a diet that is full of all the required vitamins and minerals.**

Always have seed available to your finches. This will allow them to snack whenever they feel hungry.

your pet store. Aviary birds will of course have some access to minerals that are in the aviary, but an additional supply is always beneficial. Calcium is an important mineral for breeding birds and can be supplied via oyster or egg shell, by cuttlefish bone, or via powder that is sprinkled onto damp soft- or greenfoods.

FEEDING DISHES

There are many food containers you can choose from at your pet store. These will be either open dishes or automatic feeders. It is a matter of personal preference which you

feel is best. If you choose automatic feeders select one with a wide dispenser. This reduces the risk of seed blocking the hole. Make a habit of tapping dispensers each day to ensure that the seed is falling into the holding tray. If you keep large finches, bear in mind that small dispensers will not readily release sunflower and similar large seeds - they will block the hole.

If you have a lot of birds it is wise to use open food pots. This may seem to involve more work but enables you to supply each seed type in its own container. This will be cost efficient. If you only have a few pet finches then the small amount of seed wastage will not add up to any significant sum. Birds tend to throw away seed which does not appeal to them - this can be quite an item if you have a lot of birds, which is why separate food dishes become worthwhile.

Not all finches will readily accept a new food the first time it is offered. Experiment with different types of seeds and fruits to see what your birds like.

The feeder pots should be placed close to a perch so the birds can eat from them easily. Some finches are natural ground feeders, and seed scattered on the floor, or in pots on the floor, is beneficial. Always blow the husks away from open food pots each day. If you do not, it can look as though the dish is still full of seed when it actually only contains husks.

WHEN TO FEED

Seed must always be available to your finches. Softfood and other items can be supplied in the morning, or in the late afternoon. This is important where aviary birds are concerned because it means they have time to eat these before the strong heat of the midday sun starts to dry out or sour the food. Establish a routine that suits your workday and try to stick with it.

SUITABLE SEEDS

The basic seed ration for finches will be made up of canary seed and panicum millet. Both are rich in carbohydrates, which provide the birds with energy for their day to day needs. Other carbohydrate rich seeds are maize, wheat and any other cereal seed. Young birds, as well as breeding adults, also need a supply of protein and fat rich seeds. Examples of these are rape, niger, maw, linseed, hemp, peanuts (unsalted), and

23

sunflower. Peanuts and sunflower are too large for small finches to cope with unless they are crushed to a manageable size.

Protein and fat seeds help to build body tissue and provide a layer of fat insulation so the birds are more able to cope with colder weather. A layer of fat is not so important with birds maintained indoors, so supply these accordingly otherwise they may become obese. Not all birds like all of the seeds mentioned, it is a case of trying a few and see how they take to them. Panicum on the ear in the form of millet

sprays are relished by all birds, but use them only as a treat otherwise they may ignore other needed seeds.

If seeds are soaked in tepid, fresh water for 24-36 hours, and then rinsed, you will find a new, nutritious, well-liked treat. They are especially useful for ailing birds, young stock, and those which are recovering from an illness. The seeds become richer in vitamins and are easier for the birds to digest. However, any not eaten within a short time must be discarded as they quickly deteriorate.

The seeding heads of grasses,

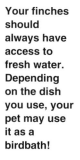

Your finches should always have access to fresh water. Depending on the dish you use, your pet may use it as a birdbath!

Finches can be fed a variety of foods, including seeds, small pieces of fruits and vegetables, some plants, and even live foods. There are several types of commercially-prepared bird foods on the market.

numerous flowers, and many wild plants are greatly favored by finches, and can be supplied when in season. Always rinse wild plants because they may carry pesticides or motor vehicle pollutants which could be toxic.

OTHER FOODS

The range of other foods that your finches will enjoy is very extensive. You can chop up small pieces of most fruits and vegetables. Whole plants, such as dandelion, shepherd's purse, coltsfoot, chickweed, and thistles will all be pecked over with interest. Avoid any plants you are not sure about in respect to their toxicity. Bread soaked in milk, hard-boiled egg yolk, cheese, beef extracts, whole wheat bread crumbs, and any similar products, are all useful for making mashes for the birds. You can purchase canary rearing and protein rich foods from your pet store; these are well recommended for breeding birds and young stock. Livefood is useful for many species, but not essential if you feed commercial protein softfoods. You can purchase a range of livefoods, or their cultures, from pet shops if you keep species known to need

**Melba Finch,
*Pytilia melba
melba*.
Melba Finches
are calm and
ideal aviary
birds. They are
usually neither
shy nor
aggressive
with other
birds. Males
will often show
aggressiveness
towards each
other if they
are competing
for a mate.**

these during the breeding period.

Birds are of course creatures of habit, and may ignore a food they have never previously tasted. This being so, do not assume they don't like a given item just because they left it the first time it was offered. Persevere with various items, and mix them with foods they enjoy. The greater the variety of food they take, the less the chance some important vitamin will be missing from their diet. Never be afraid to experiment a little.

ADDITIVES

There are numerous vitamin rich additives and tonic seeds produced for finches, but use these with caution. If your birds eat a varied diet they will lack nothing. Excess vitamins can be as dangerous as not having enough. However, such supplements are beneficial if your finches have not yet developed a taste for a wide variety of foodstuffs. Common sense is the keyword to success in most aspects of birdkeeping.

Breeding

The breeding of finch-like birds is a fascinating aspect of the hobby, but should not be undertaken on a casual basis. Even the so-called "well established" breeding species can present many problems to the beginner. This so, the first advice is that you should not think in terms of breeding your birds until you have gained at least a few months (ideally a full season) of experience at keeping them. In this way you will get to know them and their feeding habits, and can utilize the time in obtaining nest boxes, stock cages and the like. You will also have the time to ponder, which birds should be paired together for the best results.

Zebra Finch, *Poephila guttata*. Zebra Finches often leave their owners rather frustrated with their tendency to over-produce, however, they are joyful and amusing birds with a very pleasant appearance.

The beak of the Melba Finch, *Pytilia melba*, is long, pointed, and red. The color in females is usually less bright.

THE BREEDING SEASON

The breeding season for those living in temperate climates will be the spring through summer months. Where birds are maintained indoors in flights or cages the breeding season can, in reality, be throughout the year. This is because you can "fool" the birds by supplying artificial daylight, warmth, and the needed foods that would normally only be available during the natural breeding period. However, even if you are able to supply artificial conditions it is best to conduct your first breedings during the spring and summer months.

NEST BOXES AND STOCK CAGES

The two needed items for your breeding endeavors are nest boxes and one or more stock cages. The type of nest box required depends upon the species you are keeping. The stock cages will be essential to house the young stock once they fledge and leave the nest. At such a time the parents normally proceed to rear another clutch of chicks.

Nest boxes will be one of three basic types:

1. Open pan type. This is used by canaries and a few other finch species. It consists of a shallow plastic dish in which a felt pad is placed. The birds will use this as a base and build a shallow, simple, open nest on it.

2. Nest basket. This is a domed wicker structure with a hole in the front just below the roof. Once again, this will form the base structure in which the birds will fashion the actual nest.

3. Nest box. This is simply a wooden cube or oblong in which an opening or hole is placed in the front. A landing perch is fitted below the hole. The roof should be hinged to form a lid so that you can inspect the nest and the chicks without undue problems. The opening or hole should be just large enough for the adults to enter. You can obtain each of the nest types from a pet shop, or you could make your own, especially the box type. An outdoor nest box should be made of more substantial timber than one for indoors, it must be capable of resisting damp, cold, and hot periods.

Choose the aviary nest box site with care. It should be protected from winds and rain, and most species prefer some seclusion in the form of aviary plantings close to the nest. Always use more nest boxes than there are pairs of birds. This reduces the risk of squabbling. Likewise, place a number of boxes at similar heights, so none seem more favorably located than others - from the bird's viewpoint. When pairs seem reluctant to nest, a change in the nesting site often resolves the problem.

Supply nesting material in the form of grasses, dried mosses, artificial bedding as used for hamsters, pieces of fine raffia, strips of hessian, indeed anything small, pliable and soft. Avoid straw or hay as these can carry bacteria or fungal problems, and may also have sharp points on them. Cotton and similar materials

29

are also dangerous as they can entwine around a bird's legs or neck.

BREEDING IN BRIEF

In such a small book as this it is clearly not possible to discuss the breeding habits of finches in any sort of detail. It will provide a general guide to what you may reasonably expect to happen. Bear in mind that individual pairs may not always conform to average statistics. A finch will generally be sexually mature by the age of six months—which is not to say that breeding from such a young bird is desirable. Wait until it is at least nine months old. Mate a young bird with an older one which has already reared youngsters. Be sure both of the pair are in good, fit breeding condition—which can take a few months to achieve. Supply them with extra protein foods, as well as calcium rich items, and livefoods. Courtship in birds involves the male singing, and may include his carrying little twigs and grasses to the hen.

One or both of the pair may attend to the actual building of the nest, though often the hen does this while the male gathers materials for her. Once she has laid eggs she will be conspicuous, spending more and more time on the nest. On average, finches will lay 2-5 eggs which will be incubated by the hen (sometimes with the help of the male) for 12-14 days. Incubation may commence with the second or the last egg laid. The chicks will remain in

Green Twinspot, *Mandingoa nitidula*. As with most finch species, the female is a paler version of the male and lacks the red face patch. Instead, the facial area is dull orange.

White Headed Munia, *Lonchura maja*. The toenails of munias grow at a phenomenal rate and require frequent clipping. If this is not attended to regularly the birds can often become hung up on their cage and injure themselves.

the nest for 13-17 days, depending on the species and the temperature, this can stretch to 22 days (development takes longer in colder weather).

Once the chicks leave the nest (fledge) they will normally be fed by the male for a few days longer. In the meantime the hen will already have laid a second round of eggs which she will be incubating. Once the chicks are seen to be consuming hard seed it is best to remove them to a stock cage just in case the male begins to attack them. In the wild the independent youngsters would of course leave the nest when they no longer require their parents. In some species the youngsters can safely be left with the parents, assuming there is sufficient room for all of them in the aviary.

Once the chicks are fully independent of their parents they can be sold. However, you

Diamond Firetail, *Emblema guttata*. The Diamond Firetail Finch or Diamond Sparrow is difficult to sex, the unusual courting display is always the best indication.

should ensure that the chicks are eating seed without problem before you dispose of them. Initially, their perches should be lower than normal, and seed should be scattered on the cage floor. Once they understand they can feed from automatic feeders you can stop scattering seed. Supply them with soaked seed and soft rearing foods in the early days, so they get a good start in life on a wholesome diet.

LEGBANDS

Plastic split bands or rings can be placed onto birds of any age, but closed metal rings must be fitted when the chicks are only 5-8 days old. You must obtain the correct ring size for your species. They are sold by clubs and specialty avicultural suppliers. Most are year dated and may be made to carry your own identification numbers. If fitted, be sure to make regular checks that the rings have not become clogged with fecal matter. This could slow or cut off the blood supply to the toes. Always dampen such dirt before gently removing it a little at a time.

Exhibition

The exhibition side of birdkeeping is extremely interesting, and you are well recommended to visit a number of bird shows even if you have no desire to ultimately participate in them. You will see a large variety of finches and have the opportunity of discussing them with their breeders. Stock is also on sale at these events. A bird show can range in size from a small informal affair held by a local bird club, to a major event of the year which can be spread over two or more days. They are advertised in all of the cage and aviary bird magazines of your country.

If your interest develops into becoming a participant then do

Pied Zebra Finch, *Poephila guttata*. Pied Zebra Finches show a mottling of white against dark upperparts. This factor can occur and be noticeable in nearly any variety of Zebra Finch.

White Breasted Lady Gouldian Finch, *Chloebia gouldiae*. Lady Gouldians are very difficult birds to breed. Most often they abandon their eggs or throw newly hatched chicks from the nest. To avoid such expensive losses, it is often best to foster the Gouldian's eggs under a reliable breeder such as the Zebra Finch.

appreciate that a great deal of time and preparatory work goes into staging a good exhibition bird. It is not enough to have a good looking specimen because it is of little value if it cringes in fear in a corner of its cage when being judged. It must be a very fit bird, able to withstand the rigors of being transported to the venue, show itself well to the judge, and then be taken back home. It is a time and cost consuming matter for you - but you could restrict your activities to the local shows, so as to tailor make the hobby to fit in with your available time.

SHOW CAGES

You must have the appropriate cage in order to exhibit your finch. These fall into three broad categories. There are the special cages used for canaries, which are individual to the variety, the Zebra Finch cage which is also of a very specific shape and dimensions, and there is the general finch cage which can be used for a number of differing species. Apart from the all wire canary cages, the rest comprise of a wooden cage fitted with a finch front. The wood is painted black and the inside is of white, or a light pastel color. A show cage cannot carry any marks of identification that would suggest who its owner is. It must also be kept in spotless condition because a badly kept cage could loose you points.

SHOW BIRD PREPARATION

The exhibition bird must be in tight feather and hard condition. The plumage must therefore look immaculate. This is only possible if it is given a really sound diet - good feather comes from within rather than via sprays and other applicants that are sold for external use. The show bird must receive individual attention in the weeks that precede an exhibition. Light spraying with tepid water will help maintain good feathers in sparkling condition. Avoid handling or netting the show bird as this might damage a feather.

Training must commence with a young bird. It essentially entails getting it familiar both with the exhibition cage and the changes in its environment. Initially, from just a hour or so a day, it must be able to remain in the show cage for at least twenty-four or more hours, as will happen during a show. It must not become frightened at the sight of strangers wearing all manner of differing clothes, nor by the sight of strange

birds, nor of the general noises it will experience at an exhibition. Training therefore entails moving the bird, in its show cage, to other rooms in your home, and encouraging friends and visitors to stand near its cage to look at it. Generally, finches take quite well to exhibitions once they have a little experience. Do not over compete them otherwise they will loose condition. It will take the exhibition bird a few weeks to regain the fitness suited for breeding, so do not expect such a bird to go from

the show perch to the breeding cage or aviary without a period for it to recoup. The show season normally ends as the breeding season commences, but they do overlap.

JUDGING

A bird is either judged against an official standard, as in canaries, Zebra Finches, and a few others, or it is judged on its overall condition, size, quality of feather, and color, and then compared with the other entrants. Classes will be scheduled for males and hens (in the dimorphic species) as well as for the differing color mutations, where they are applicable. There are also classes for pairs and teams. These classes are harder because you must stage two or more birds that are comparable in size, color, markings, and so on - not just your best birds, which is not quite the same thing.

The best birds in their respective classes go on to compete for the best of their species, then for best bird of their group. Finally, all the group winners compete for the best bird in the show. Exhibiting birds is a logical conclusion to a breeding program. It enables you to compare your success in standards attained against those of other breeders. It is also a social activity in which you will meet many new friends, keep abreast of what is happening in the bird world, and make many contacts, both for buying and selling, or swapping stock.

Indian Silverbill, *Lonchura malabarica*. Not a particularly attractive bird because it does not display any vivid color markings, however, the Indian Silverbill is an inexpensive, hardy, and prolific breeding bird.

Finches in the Home

Owl Finch,
Poephila
bichenovii.
The Owl Finch
displays a
very pleasing
appearance
and has a
friendly and
delightful
personality as
well as a
peaceful
congeniality
towards all
other birds.

If you wish to enjoy the pleasure of two or more finches in your home you should endeavor to provide them with the largest cage or indoor flight that you can. In this chapter we will look at other aspects relating to pet finches.

THE LIBERTY FINCH

Although many owners deny their birds the pleasure of liberty flying in a home environment, this can be done with even the smallest of finches, providing certain precautions, and facts, are taken into consideration. The first obvious precaution is to safeguard the bird from danger and from escaping. Here are a few potential problems and safeguards:

1. Never leave an open fire unguarded - nor a chimney when the fire is, or is not, alight. Cover this with a guard mesh. This applies also to electric fires when they are in use.

2. Never leave doors open,

The Swee Waxbill, *Estrilda melanotis*, is a tiny bird which is an absolute delight to watch, for it is ever on the alert, and it is fit, full of energy and friendliness.

especially outside doors. It is best to confine the birds to one room and keep all doors in this room closed while the birds are at liberty.

3. Initially hang some curtain netting over windows. If this is not done the birds may dash themselves against the glass - with fatal results. Never, of course, leave any windows open.

4. If you have an aquarium be sure that it is fitted with a canopy so the birds do not accidentally fall in!

5. Do not allow other pets to be loose, especially cats, when the birds are free flying, otherwise pandemonium could occur.

6. Cover extractor fans with a fine mesh so the birds are in no danger of flying into these.

You cannot "potty train" finches, so be prepared to wipe up their droppings, as well as their scattered seeds. Delicate ornaments should not be placed onto shelves where they may be knocked off by a fluttering bird.

TAMING

You cannot tame a finch to the same degree that you can a parrot-like bird, but the larger finches can be finger trained if you are gentle and very patient. If they are straight from the nest youngsters this is obviously much easier. The training is done while they are in their cage by you gently placing your finger under their chest. This prompts them to hop onto it. The process is much longer than with a parrot, so only the most patient owners will be successful.

Even if they are not finger tame, your finches will return to their cage in order to feed. The more often they are allowed out, the less difficult it will be to encourage them to return to the cage. Do not let the finches out of their cage

Pied Zebra Finch, *Poephila guttata*. No two Pied Zebra Finches have exactly the same markings.

Tri-colored Munia, *Lonchura malacca*. The sexing of this bird is very difficult. In the extremes, males have larger and more masculine beaks than females. Behavior is actually the only sure sign.

until they have had a week or two in which to settle down and become familiar with their surroundings. During this period you can talk to them and feed them tidbits through the cage bars so they overcome their natural fear of humans.

GENERAL CARE

The pet finch may not shed its feathers in the same way that an aviary bird will. Aviary birds go through an annual molt in the late summer, but home pets may be in a constant state of feather loss known as a soft molt. This is due to the artificial environment it lives in. This is not a problem in most instances. When a bird is seen to be molting it will certainly help if you give it a light, daily spray with tepid water. This will equate rain, and keep the feathers supple. Feathers tend to get rather dry and brittle in the constant warm temperature of a home that may be overheated. With respect to temperatures, always try to locate the cage where it is away from the heat source, and from drafts. In this way fluctuations in temperature will be minimal. Sudden changes will quickly chill a bird which could otherwise cope with differences if they are gradual.

The nails of some finches may overgrow if their perches are not of variable thickness - and sometimes even if they are. If this proves to be the case you can easily trim the claws with sharp scissors. Be very sure not to cut close to the blood vessel, which is easily seen, otherwise the nail will bleed (not to mention be very painful to your pet).

FEEDING

The pet bird, unless given ample liberty flying, will not be getting the same amount of exercise as the aviary bird - nor will it need the same level of fat insulation to protect it from the cold. With these facts in mind do not overfeed it protein or fat rich seeds which may make it obese. Do not forget to give it some wild plants when these are available in the spring and summer. Initially, greens should be rationed. Birds enjoy these very much and a glut of any one food item will probably result in a digestive upset.

Finally, in the warmer months, it is beneficial to place the bird's cage in the early morning sunshine which it enjoys. However, always be sure that part of the cage is shaded so it can retreat from the sun's rays whenever it wishes. You can leave the cage out in light showers for a few minutes which will be invigorating, but not so long that it becomes soaked. Again a shaded area in the cage will be useful.

Green Avadavat, *Amandava formosa*. To encourage these birds to attempt breeding, a number of possible sites for the nest should be provided, and the most likely places are in thick bushes or in tall, reed-like grasses.

Health Care

Finches have a high metabolic rate. The effect of this is that if they fall ill they deteriorate very rapidly. Conversely, they can also make a dramatic recovery if treatment is prompt. Clearly, prevention is better than cure, so general management should be conducted with this in mind.

QUARANTINE

A golden rule of animal husbandry is that all newly acquired stock should be subjected to a period of quarantine. If you have never kept birds on your property before there is no specific need to quarantine them if they are to be house pets. However, if they are to be aviary birds it would be prudent to isolate them in a stock cage for a period of two weeks before releasing them into the aviary.

The object of quarantine, or isolation, is to enable you to observe the birds under controlled conditions. You can make sure the birds are eating well, and you can also control the temperature of their accommodation. If they are incubating a disease, or a treatable condition, this has time to show itself. Two weeks of isolation may not be sufficient for all diseases to manifest themselves, but most will. If the birds have been kept in a warm pet shop and you plan to place them in an aviary, the isolation period enables you to slowly acclimatize them to the lower temperatures. In such a case it would be wise to extend the period to a number of weeks. If the birds were purchased in the autumn it would be best to retain them indoors until the spring.

Red Collared Whydah, *Coliuspasser ardens ardens*. The male Red Collared Whydah is one of those birds which often does not go fully out of color or which often does not come completely into color.

GENERAL HUSBANDRY

The major cause of disease and illnesses in cage and aviary birds is, in many instances, directly attributable to poor husbandry. Pathogenic (disease causing) bacteria will gain footholds in your cage or aviary under the following conditions:

1. Feeding dishes that are not cleaned daily, or not replaced when cracked or showing signs of wear.

2. Perches that are not kept clean and replaced when showing signs of wear.

3. Cage or aviary floors (especially) and walls that are not cleaned on a weekly basis.

4. Overcrowding stock. Direct transmission of bacteria and parasites from one bird to another

is an obvious high risk when birds are forced to perch tightly against one another.

5. Stress. When birds are intimidated by larger or aggressive birds they use up nervous energy. This will make them more vulnerable to ailments that would ordinarily not be a problem. Stress can also be caused by cats, dogs, noises, and indeed very many environmental situations, so it is not an easy condition to identify.

6. Poor quality and unclean foods. Always ensure that your birds' food is of the best quality, never tainted, and it should be stored in airtight containers.

7. Extremes of temperature. Cold weather induces chills, especially when accompanied by dampness. Very hot weather

Zebra Finch, *Poephila guttata*. The Zebra Finch is a very agreeable bird that does well in any environment. They do not require any special care nor livefood. Breeding is very easy.

44

results in bacteria being able to multiply more readily. If these situations are combined with other negative husbandry aspects they clearly compound matters.

8. Lack of quarantining newly acquired birds. Once you have birds that are fit and healthy you take the great risk of introducing bacteria to these if additional birds are not screened for good health. Many aviary owners have lost a number of birds (sometimes all of them) because a newcomer carrying a disease was not quarantined.

IDENTIFYING A PROBLEM

The following are signs of an illness:

1. A discharge of mucus or liquid from the eyes or nostrils.

2. Any crusty, scale-like appearance to the beak, face, or legs. Raised scales on the legs.

3. Any bald areas on the body.

4. Very liquid fecal matter, especially if it is blood-streaked.

5. Difficulty if breathing.

6. Perching with feathers fluffed up and standing on both legs with head drooped.

7. Lack of interest in food.

8. Lack of normal activity.

To recognize any of these signs you must of course spend some time each day watching your finches so that you become familiar with all of their habits. Once you have decided that one or more finches have a problem you should make notes on the clinical signs, as well as on the conditions under which they live, their diet, ambient temperature, how long owned, where purchased, and so on. The more detail you keep, the more it will help your vet make a diagnosis.

Essentially, problems will be

either external, caused by parasites, or internal, caused by bacteria, viruses or fungi. External problems are easier to treat because it is often possible to identify the causal organism. Internal problems are more difficult, and can often only be diagnosed from blood or fecal samples after microscopy. Unfortunately, by the time tests can be completed, the patient has probably died in many instances. In such cases it is wise to have an autopsy. This might identify the disease, and other birds may be saved by the appropriate treatment.

TREATING AILING FINCHES

The potential ways in which an ailing finch can be treated are threefold. Firstly, heat treatment often works wonders for non-specific problems, as well as being

Diamond Firetail, *Emblema guttata*. When these birds are kept in a cage indoors rather than in an aviary, they tend to become rather lethargic and eat until they become overly fat.

Green Twinspot, *Mandingoa nitidula*. This magnificent finch frequents dense brush and thorn tangles on river banks and spends most of its time on the ground among thick undergrowth. When keeping these birds in an aviary, it is a good idea to have some shrubbery in the aviary with the birds.

essential for any identified conditions. Secondly, antibiotics can be administered either in the drinking water, or on the food. Finally, medicines, in ointment or liquid form, can be applied directly to the skin. The oral administration of medicines may also be possible with larger finches, but may induce shock (through handling) in the smaller species.

Visible external parasites, such as feather and skin mites, will not need specific heat treatment. The bird(s) should be isolated from other stock, so the parasites do not spread. At the same time, all of the accommodation and utensils should be thoroughly cleaned and treated, otherwise the birds will become reinfected. Skin parasites only survive and spread in unclean conditions.

For most internal ailments, heat should form part of the treatment. This accelerates the condition and renders the causal pathogens more susceptible to attack by antibiotics. A simple, yet effective, hospital cage can be made using a stock cage and an infrared lamp. The lamp is placed near one end of the cage, or clamped to it (depending on the model). If a thermostat is built into this, all the better. You want to maintain a temperature of about 90°F (32°C). Using a stock cage enables the patient to move away from the heat source if it feels uncomfortable. The cage used to accommodate an ill bird must of course be spotlessly clean. It should be fitted with a thermometer at each end so the temperature can be monitored. Do not supply fruits if medication is to be placed in the water. The bird will then be encouraged to drink. Seed must always be available, and soaked seed is often a valuable food for ill and recovering birds. Lower the perches so they are closer to the floor. A finch will normally

recover (if it is going to) within a few days with heat and other treatments. Continue, however, with the full treatment as prescribed by your veterinarian, otherwise a relapse may occur. Once a bird is on the mend it is essential to acclimatize it back to its normal housing temperature. Never rush this. Do not place a recovered bird back into an aviary during inclement weather periods, nor of course if you feel there is any chance that the causal problem has not been totally rectified.

Do not attempt to treat an

The distinctive characteristic of the Orange-cheeked Waxbill, *Estrilda melpoda*, is the orange-yellow patch on the cheeks. Some birds have a larger patch than others, but it is not safe to assume that all birds with the largest patches are males.

The Black-headed Munia, *Lonchura malacca*, is a trimly shaped bird that is frequently kept in an aviary. They are gregarious and peaceful in nature.

ailing bird until the problem has been identified. This may make matters worse, and allows the problem to reach a more advanced, and maybe untreatable, state. In this chapter it has not been possible to discuss specific diseases and conditions, only how to avoid them, or to take remedial actions. Only your vet can identify and treat internal disorders. External parasites can be treated with proprietary medicines from pet shops or your vet, once you have correctly advised them of the clinical signs.

Popular Finch Species

There are thousands of finches and finch-like species of birds, but only about one hundred of these are commonly kept in aviculture. Less than half of these could be considered species suited to the first time birdkeeper. The species discussed in this chapter range from the very popular to those which would generally be regarded as the limits a beginner should attempt to keep.

The descriptions of the species are very basic. The color photographs throughout this book do more justice to colors and patterns than words could ever do. When you read of one or more finches that are of interest, you are advised to seek a more detailed text on these. The species covered are not discussed in family order, but based on their relative popularity. The scientific standing of the species and their zoological taxonomy is an important and interesting subject, but is beyond the scope of this book. It is especially useful if you plan to collect and breed on a more

Opposite: **Longtailed Grassfinch,** *Poephila acuticauda.* **The Grassfinch is an ideal aviary bird. It is hardy, peaceful, and requires simple care. It is a very active bird that adds beauty to any aviary.**

than casual basis. Sizes quoted are approximate averages given purely as a basic guide.

CANARY, *Serinus canaria* 5.5in (14cm)

Although you may not regard this as an exotic finch, it is nonetheless a true finch of the family Fringillidae. Canaries make delightful cage or aviary birds, and the males have quite beautiful songs. The most popular color is yellow, but there are greens, browns, whites, and a whole range of pastel shades, such as rose, cinnamon, and silver. Canaries make great pet birds, and also very colorful additions to the aviary. The most popular variety is the Border Fancy. Price depends on the variety and quality, but pet specimens are very reasonable. An open nestpan is the preferred choice for breeding.

GREEN & GRAY SINGING FINCHES, GENUS *Serinus* 11.5cm (4.5in)

These two finch species are the most readily available of a number of related species found

from southern Europe through Africa. They are hardy birds once acclimatized, and though not especially colorful, are aviary favorites on account of their sweet song. In this respect, the Gray Singing Finch (*S.leucopygius*), while a more somber color, has the sweeter song. The prettier Green species (*S.mozambicus*) - actually almost yellow - is nonetheless a very capable songster. When breeding, allow these birds plenty of space. They are good residents in a mixed finch collection and are modestly priced.

ZEBRA FINCH *Poephila guttata* 11.5cm (4.5in)

Originally a bird of the arid regions of Australia, this little waxbill (so called for the red wax-like beak) is the most popular of all "foreign finches." It is a hardy bird that offers good breeding potential, a number of established color mutations, a very pleasing wild type color pattern, and a delightful, friendly personality. It is quite safe in a mixed collection. In its wild type color pattern the Zebra Finch is just about the least expensive of any finch species - mutational colors, as well as crested birds and yellow beaks, are slightly more costly. This is a very

Yellow Mantled Whydah, *Coliuspasser macrourus*. A male in nuptial plumage.

popular exhibition bird. It is recommended very highly for the novice. For breeding, a wicker basket or a wooden nesting box is preferred. The male can be recognized by the barring on his throat, the orange cheek patches, and the white spotted chestnut flank markings, all of which are absent in the hen.

SOCIETY FINCH, *Lonchura domestica* 10cm (4in)

This highly popular finch is believed to be the domesticated form of the White-backed munia (*L. striata*) which is native to Asia. Although the Society is not as colorful as the Zebra Finch, it makes up for this by being a very

accommodating and friendly bird. It breeds readily in a cage or aviary, and is the first choice by those who want a bird to foster other finch species' eggs or young, such as the Gouldian. This species uses either a wooden nest box or a wicker basket. The sexes are similar but the cock has a sweet warbling song when courting a mate. The Society is one of the most modestly priced finches. A number of color mutations are available.

Black Crowned Waxbill, *Estrilda nonnula*. The Black Crowned Waxbill is a delightful bird to include in any aviary because of its bright and cheerful personality as well as a very attractive and unusual pattern.

THE NUNS, GENUS *Lonchura* 11.5cm (4.5in)

There are three popular little finches known as nuns or mannikins, these being the White-headed (*L.maja*), the Black-headed (*L.malacca*), and the Tri-colored (also *L.malacca*). They are also known as munias, and are but three of numerous similar birds in which black, brown, and white are the colors. When breeding they prefer a domed wicker basket as the base for the nest. They are hardy birds and long time aviary favorites. They are moderately priced and the sexes are similar.

In the three species mentioned of the genus Lonchura, note that black, brown, and white are the basic colors. There are a number of other popular aviary birds in this genus in which these colors predominate. The Spice Finch (*L. punctualata*) is brown with its chest and underparts having a scalloped effect of white edged with brown. They are a modestly priced species and hardy once acclimatized. Sexes are similar.

The Silverbills of Africa and Asia are two other popular and

low priced finches housed in the *Lonchura* genus. Rather less common is the Pearl-headed Silverbill (*L.caniceps*). This species has more pleasing colors than many *Lonchura* species, adding gray to the colors listed for the genus. It also sports white spots on its facial area. Sexes are similar. Nesting requirements are the same as for other munias or mannikins.

CUTTHROAT, *Amadina fasciata* 12.5cm (5in)

Named for the splash of bright red across the throat of the male (not present on the hen), this is yet another long-time aviary favorite that can be purchased at a modest sum. They are not bred in large numbers, but will readily nest in wooden nest boxes or domed baskets. Once carefully acclimatized they are hardy birds in the aviary. Some are fine with smaller finches, but others can be aggressive, and therefore are best placed with other species, such as Java Sparrows, small weavers, and their like, which can take care of themselves. They are a good choice for the beginner.

JAVA SPARROW *Padda oryzivora* **14cm (5.5in)**

With its black cap, white cheeks and gray body, the Java Sparrow always looks immaculate. It is a highly popular cage and aviary bird being bold, and hardy when acclimatized. It is a self

Left: Blue-headed Cordon Bleu, *Uraeginthus cyanocephalus.* The male of this species is very distinctive in that the entire head and neck are blue instead of brown on top of the head and nape.

assertive bird that can be a bit of a bully if placed with small or delicate finches. In a mixed collection it should be included with weavers, Cutthroats, and similar birds that are not easily intimidated. When breeding, a wooden nest box will be fine. There are a few color mutations, such as the white and the fawn and these help to make the species a good exhibition prospect. The sexes are similar. The Java will cost you a little more than the more common finches, but is still modestly priced for what you are getting.

POPULAR AFRICAN WAXBILLS

Africa is home to a number of very popular little finches that are both colorful and modest to moderate in price. Once acclimatized they are quite hardy, though background heat is advised in birdrooms during the winter period. A trio of broadly similar birds are the Orange-cheeked Waxbill (*Estrilda melpoda*), the Red-eared Waxbill (*E. troglodytes*) and the St. Helena, or Common Waxbill. Each has a bright red beak and is shades of grays, browns, and white. The Red-eared Waxbill and the Common Waxbill have streaks of red running from the beak through the eyes to the neck. The sexes are similar.

Rather more costly is the Lavender Finch (*Estrilda caerulescens*) with its dark beak, lavender body and crimson

Opposite: Red-headed Lady Gouldian, *Chloebia gouldiae.* From the shape of the bill, one could easily see that the Gouldian is an eater of small grass seeds. They also eat a great deal of insectivorous foods during their breeding season.

57

rump and tail. This species must be carefully acclimatized if it is a recent import.

Always a favorite is the tiny, 9cm (3.5in), Gold-breasted Waxbill (*Amandava subflava*). Quite hardy once well acclimatized, this is a chirpy little species that has a good breeding record, especially if it has its own aviary. The male has a red eye stripe lacking in the hen. Wicker baskets or open fronted wooden nest boxes are favored nesting sites.

Moving to more costly species of African waxbills there are the Cordon Bleus of the genus *Uraeginthus*. These are essentially blue and brown birds, though the males of one species are red cheeked. In length they are about 12.5cm (5in). They are popular exhibition birds and well established in captivity. The beak is a dull red-brown color. Wicker baskets or open wooden nest boxes will be used if the birds are unable to build their own nests in a shrub in the aviary - this being true of most of the African finches. Closely related to the Cordon Bleus are the beautiful Purple Grenadier (*U. ianthinogaster*) and the Violet-eared Waxbill (*U. granatina*). They are more costly. Although tempting birds to own, the novice is advised to leave them until experience has been gained because they can be delicate, as well as somewhat aggressive in mixed company.

Other popular African

Red-cheeked Cordon Bleu, *Uraeginthus bengalus*. Cordon Bleus are often responsible for kindling the first interest in many bird fanciers because they are so charming and pretty that they are often the first to catch the eye of newcomers.

waxbills will include the numerous species of Fire Finches. These are so-called for the various amounts of red in their plumage. Sexes are similar, though males are often more reddish on the back. They are hardy birds of modest cost and will breed well once established in an aviary.

Red-billed Fire-finch, *Lagonosticta senegala.* Fire finches spend a great part of time near the ground and are happy in a planted aviary.

GOULDIAN FINCH,
Chloebia gouldiae **12.5cm (5in)**

No book on finches could fail to mention the Gouldian Finch. This species ranks as one of the world's most beautiful avians. With red, black, purple, gold, orange, and blue green in distinct areas of its body, this is a bird that always commands attention. It is a highly popular exhibition bird as well as being a favorite pet in many homes. However, while not difficult to maintain, it is not a finch the novice should begin breeding with until experienced. A high percentage of chicks have to be fostered by other finch species because the parents do not have good rearing backgrounds. The Gouldian must be given heated quarters during the winter months because, like a number of other Australian finches, it cannot be regarded as being very hardy (the Zebra Finch being one of the notable exceptions to this comment). There are a number of color mutations apart from the natural color forms of red-headed, black-headed, and yellow- (orange) headed. As you might expect, this is a rather expensive species to purchase.

OTHER AUSTRALIAN FINCHES

There are a number of Australian grassfinches which are highly popular and

Red Headed Lady Gouldian, *Chloebia gouldiae*. In comparison to the male, the female Lady Gouldian shows much variation in the amount of red on the head.

desirable cage and aviary birds. Generally, they are better suited to the aviary, or large indoor flight, than to confinement in cage. Some are quite ready breeders while others may prove very selective in the partners they choose. All of these birds will have been bred in captivity because their export from Australia was banned in 1959. Their cost ranges from moderate to very expensive, especially where mutational colors are concerned. However, it should not be assumed that mutational colors are prettier than the wild colors (often this is not so). It is their rarity that makes them valuable. Keep the following finches in a warm environment during the cold and damp weather. Although the colors of brown, black and white may not seem especially exciting, they are when seen on the Bicheno or Owl Finch (*Poephila bichenovii*). With a fine black line masking the white face, white spots on the wings, and the silver beak, this little finch is a real eye-catcher. It can be bred on a colony system. Sexes are similar. The Longtailed Grassfinch (*Poephila acuticauda*) is another super little bird with its orange-yellow beak, black throat spot, gray head, and soft shades of fawn on the body. It is a reliable breeder and usually a good mixer with other finches. The red beaked form is known as Heck's Grassfinch.

The Diamond Sparrow or Firetail (*Emblema guttata*) is yet

another very pleasing Australian finch. The red beak and rump, and the black chest bar over white underparts contrast nicely. There is a black eye stripe which ends at the red eye ring to add to the appeal of this popular bird. Some of the species are very placid in mixed company, but others are the opposite.

WEAVERS & WHYDAHS

You will no doubt see a number of weavers and whydahs in pet shops and on dealers listings, but these birds are not really ideal avians for the novice, nor are many suited to life as a cage bird (though they may make ideal exhibition birds). They are easily sexed because the male undergoes a plumage change when the breeding season approaches - he adorns his nuptial feathers. These are usually highly colorful compared to the out of season colors of dull browns, which are the hen's year round colors. These birds can become very aggressive and are therefore not suited to residence in a mixed collection

Longtailed Grassfinch, *Poephila acuticauda*. Longtailed Grassfinches help to enhance the reputation of all Australian finches because they are ideal breeders, however, the conditions must favor them before they show any interest.

of small finches, though solitary males are usually not a problem. Most of the weavers and whydahs are parasitic when breeding. This means they lay their eggs in the nests of other birds, who then rear them as their own. Most species have a particular host, so unless you have that species, and they are also breeding, you cannot breed with the parasitic species - which is why these are difficult birds to cater for as breeding propositions.

Among the more popular species are the Pin-tailed Whydah (*Vidua macroura*). This little bird is only 11.5cm (4.5in) in length, but in nuptial feather it sports a 25cm (10in) tail. It has a red beak and is black and white in color - and very aggressive for its small size. A suitable aviary companion for the Pin-tailed would be the Orange or Red Bishop (*Euplectes orix*), which has a length of about 12.5cm. This is a weaver finch from Africa and the nests built by weavers are variable from modest to very elaborate. In full color the Bishop has a red-orange ruff of feathers around its neck which contrast with the black of the head and underparts. When breeding it should be placed with several hens otherwise it may persecute a single female. Another colorful weaver of similar size is the Napoleon (*Euplectes afra*), which is black, yellow, and brown in color. Its breeding habits are similar to the Red Bishop. For best results, both species should be given their own aviary.

Within this chapter only a very small sampling has been given of the range finches you may purchase. However, the most popular have been discussed and should give you plenty to choose from. Remember that it is unwise to mix birds of differing size unless you know the larger species to be very placid. Likewise, and especially when breeding, avoid mixing species of similar colors and nesting sites.

With the proper care, a finch can be a happy, colorful addition to your home for many years.

Index

Page numbers in boldface **refer to illustrations.**